Olga Alekseevna Novikova

Is Russia Wrong?

A series of Letters by a russian Lady

Olga Alekseevna Novikova

Is Russia Wrong?
A series of Letters by a russian Lady

ISBN/EAN: 9783337299170

Printed in Europe, USA, Canada, Australia, Japan

Cover: Foto ©ninafisch / pixelio.de

More available books at **www.hansebooks.com**

IS RUSSIA WRONG?

IS RUSSIA WRONG?

A Series of Letters,

BY

A RUSSIAN LADY,

WITH A PREFACE

BY

J. A. FROUDE, M.A.

London:
HODDER AND STOUGHTON,
27, PATERNOSTER ROW.

MDCCCLXXVII.

Printed by Hazell, Watson, and Viney, London and Aylesbury.

𝔗𝔬 𝔱𝔥𝔢 𝔐𝔢𝔪𝔬𝔯𝔶 𝔬𝔣

NICOLAS KIRÉEFF,

THE FIRST RUSSIAN VOLUNTEER KILLED IN

SERVIA, JULY $\frac{6}{18}$, 1876,

THESE LETTERS ARE DEDICATED.

PREFACE.

VERY few words will suffice for an introduction of the following letters. The writer is a Russian lady well acquainted with England, who has seen with regret the misconceptions which she considers prevail among us as to the character of her countrymen; she has therefore employed such skill as she possesses in an honourable attempt to remove them. Individuals, however great their opportunities, can but speak with certainty of what they personally know, and "O. K." may draw too wide inferences from the experiences of her own circle ; but she writes in good faith, and any contribution to our knowledge, which is true as far as it goes, ought to be welcome to us, — welcome to us especially at the present crisis, when the wise or unwise conduct of English statesmen may effect incalculably for good or evil the fortunes of many millions of mankind. To Russia and England has fallen the task of introducing European civilization into Asia. It is a thankless labour at the best; but circumstances have forced an obligation upon both of us, which neither they nor we can relinquish; and our success depends for its character on the relations which we can establish between ourselves. If we can work harmoniously together as for a common object, the progress of the Asiatic people will be peaceful and rapid. If we are to be jealous rivals, watching each other's movements with suspicion, and on the look-out to thwart and defeat each other, every kingdom and tribe from the Bosphorus to the Wall of China will be a centre of intrigue; and the establishment of the new order of things may be retarded for centuries, or disgraced by wars and revolutions from which we shall all alike be sufferers. On the broadest grounds, therefore, it is our interest to be on good terms with Russia, unless there is something in the Muscovite proceedings so unqualifiedly bad that we are positively obliged to separate ourselves from them. And before arriving at such a conclusion we must take more pains than we have done hitherto to know what the Russians are. If we could "crumple" them up as Mr. Cobden spoke of doing, we might prefer to reign in the East without a rival. But "crumpling up" is a long process, in which nothing is certain but the expense of it. That enterprise we shall certainly not attempt. There remains, therefore, the alternative: either to settle into an attitude of fixed hostility to a Power which will always exist side by side by us, or to place on Russia's action towards the Asiatic races the same favourable construction which we allow to our own, and to ask ourselves whether in Russia's conduct there is anything materially different from what we too accept as necessary in similar circumstances.

The war of 1854 was a first step in what I considered then, and consider now, to have been the wrong course—a course leading direct, if persisted in, to most deplorable issues. That war had been made inevitable from the indignation of the Liberal party throughout Europe at Russia's interference in Hungary. Professedly a war in defence of Turkey, it was fought really for European liberty. European liberty is no longer in danger, nor has the behaviour of Turkey since the peace been of a kind to give her a claim on our interest for her own sake. The Ottoman Empire has for half a century existed upon sufferance. An independence accompanied with a right of interference by other nations with its internal administration has lost its real meaning, and the great Powers have been long agreed that the Porte cannot be left to govern its Christian subjects after its own pleasure. The question is merely in whom the right of supervision is to reside. Before the Crimean war they were under the sole protectorate of Russia. The Treaty of Paris abolished an exclusive privilege which was considered dangerous, and substituted for it, by implication, a general European protectorate. It seemed likely to many of us that while other objects of the war might have been secured, the real occasion of it would be forgotten; that the Christians, having no longer Russia to appeal to, would be worse treated than before; and that after a very few years the problem of how to compel the

Turk to respect his engagements would certainly return. Such anticipations, in the enthusiasm of the moment, were ridiculed as absurd and unpatriotic. The Turk himself was to rise out of the war regenerate, and a "new creature." He was to be the advanced guard of enlightenment, the bulwark of Europe against barbarism. There was no measure to the hopes in which English people indulged in those days of delight and excitement. But facts have gone their natural way. The Turk has gone back, not forward. He remains what he has always been, a blight upon every province on which he has set his heel. His Christian subjects have appealed once more for help, and the great Powers, England included, have admitted the justice of their complaints, and the necessity of a remedy. Unhappily England could not agree with the other Powers on the nature of the remedy required. Russia, unable to trust further to promises so often made and so uniformly broken, has been obliged to take active measures, and at once the Crimean ashes have again been blown into a flame; there is a cry that Russia has sinister aims of her own, that English interests are in danger, and that we must rush to the support of our ancient friend and ally. How we are decently to do it, under what plea, and for what purpose, after the part which we took at the Conference, is not explained. The rest of Europe is not alarmed. The rest of Europe is satisfied that the Turk must be coerced, and looks on, if not pleased, yet at least indifferent. If we go into the struggle we must go in without a single ally, and when we have succeeded in defeating Russia, and re-establishing Turkey (there is another possibility, that we may not succeed, but this I will not contemplate),—as soon as we have succeeded, what then? After the censures to which we stand committed on Turkey's misconduct we cannot in decency hand back Bulgaria to her without some check upon her tyranny. We shall be obliged to take the responsibility on ourselves. England will have to be sole protector of the Bulgarian Christians, and it is absolutely certain that they would then be wholly and entirely at the Turk's mercy. It is absolutely certain that we should be contracting obligations which we could not fulfil if we wished. We should demand a few fine promises from the Porte, which would be forgotten as soon as made. A British protectorate is too ridiculous to be thought of, and if the alternative be to place Bulgaria under a government of its own, that is precisely the thing which Russia is trying to do. To go to war with such a dilemma staring us in the face, and with no object which we can distinctly define, would be as absurd an enterprise as England was ever entangled in. Yet even after Lord Derby's seeming recognition of the character of the situation, there is still room for misgiving. In constitutional countries politicians will snatch at passing gusts of popular excitement to win a momentary victory for themselves or their party. Our Premier, unless he has been misrepresented, has dreamt of closing his political career with a transformation scene,—Europe in flames behind him, and himself posing like Harlequin before the footlights. Happily there is a power which is stronger than even Parliamentary majorities,—in public opinion; and public opinion has, I trust, already decided that English bayonets shall not be stained again in defence of Turkish tyranny. It will be well if we can proceed, when the present war is over, to consider dispassionately the wider problems, of which the Turkish difficulty is only a part; and if the letters of "O. K." assist ever so little in making us acquainted with the Russian character, the writer will have reason to congratulate herself on so happy a result of her efforts.

J. A. F.

December, 1877.

⁎ *A portion of the profits of this work will be devoted to the Russian Sick and Wounded Fund.*

CONTENTS.

		PAGE
I.	SECRET SOCIETIES AND THE WAR	17
II.	THE TWO RUSSIAS — MOSCOW AND ST. PETERSBURG	29
III.	COMPENSATION FOR SACRIFICES	41
IV.	TERMS OF PEACE—POSSIBLE AND IMPOSSIBLE	53
V.	WHY RUSSIANS HATE THE TURKS	66
VI.	SOME ENGLISH PREJUDICES	77
VII.	TRADITIONAL POLICY	93
VIII.	RUSSIANS IN CENTRAL ASIA	103
IX.	MR. FORBES' ARTICLE	113
X.	M. KATKOFF AND THE "MOSCOW GAZETTE"	125

LETTER I.

SECRET SOCIETIES AND THE WAR.

IS RUSSIA WRONG?

LETTER I.

SECRET SOCIETIES AND THE WAR.

[*The following letter is an answer to an article signed "N."
in "Macmillan's Magazine," Nov.* 1877, *which contained
in a small compass most of the misstatements concerning the origin of the war, current in hostile circles.*]

LORD SALISBURY recently advised the victims of the baseless scare of a Russian invasion of India to buy large-sized maps and learn how insuperable are the obstacles which nature has placed between the land of the Czar and the dominions of the Empress. Would it be too presumptuous in a Russian to express a wish that Englishmen would pay a little attention to the history of their own country in the days of the great Elizabeth, before attempting to pronounce an opinion upon the action of the Russian people in this war? Perhaps the discovery that only three centuries ago the heroism and enthusiasm of the English Protestants anticipated in Holland and France the course taken last year by the newly-awakened enthusiasm of the Russian people in Bulgaria and Servia would moderate the vehemence of their censure, even if it did not secure for my countrymen the sympathy which Englishmen used to feel for those who are willing to sacrifice all, even life itself, in the cause of Liberty and Right.

Without sympathy understanding is impossible. Prejudice closes the door against all explanation. But no one who had entered into the spirit of the times when Sir Philip Sydney went forth to fight in the Low Countries, and Francis Drake swept the Spanish Main, could possibly have made so many grotesque blunders as those which are to be found in an article in *Macmillan's Magazine* for November, entitled, "Pan-Slavists and the Slav Committees," and signed "N." It is not very difficult to understand the source of "N.'s" inspiration. Instead of ascertaining the objects of the Slavophiles from their own lips, he has repeated all the stupid calumnies wherewith our enemies have vainly attempted to prejudice our Czar against the Slav cause. That is not fair. If a Russian writer were to describe the operations of the Eastern Question Association and Mr. Gladstone from the slanders of the English Turkophiles, he would not err more from the truth than does this English writer who caricatures the Slav Committees by repeating the calumnies of some of our official enemies.

"The Slav Committees," says "N.," "have brought about this war,"—an accusation of which I am proud, for the only alternative to war was a selfish abandonment of our Southern brethren to the merciless vengeance of the Turks. But when he says that we brought it about in order "to crush Russia in its present form of Government, the absolute rule of the Czar," he states that which is not only untrue, but what is known to be an absurdity by every Slavophile in Russia. The statement is even more absurd than the assertion made by Lord Beaconsfield that the Servian war was made by the Secret Societies. The Slavonic Committees are not secret, and they are certainly not composed of Revolutionists. It used to be the reproach of the Slav party that it was in all things too Conservative. Now we are told that we are Radicals who hate the present form of the Russian State. Both reproaches can hardly be true. As a matter of fact both are false. " N." charges M. Aksakoff with being, as President of the Moscow Committee, the head-centre of revolutionary Russia. As one of M. Aksakoff's numerous friends, I may be permitted to say that there never was a more monstrous assertion. M. Aksakoff, although no courtier, is devotedly loyal. His wife was our Empress's lady-in-waiting, and governess to the Duchess of Edinburgh; and he himself, although abused in the Turkophile papers as a Russian Mazzini, is one of the last men in the world to undertake a crusade against the Czardom. Simple, honest, enthusiastic, M. Aksakoff is no conspirator; he is simply the leading spokesman of the Russian Slavs, by whom he was elected to the post of President of the Moscow Slavonic Committee with only one dissentient voice. Much surprise was expressed that there should be even one vote against his appointment. But that surprise was succeeded by a smile when it was announced that the solitary dissentient was M. Aksakoff himself. So far from aiming at the destruction of Russian State, they aim at the much less ambitious and more useful task of emancipating their Southern brethren from Turkish oppression. There is no mystery about the operations of our committees. Their work is prosaic in the extreme. Brought into existence long ago by the operation of the same benevolent spirit which leads English people to send tracts to Fiji cannibals, these committees laboured unnoticed and unseen until the close of 1875. At that time occurred the great revolt of the Southern Slavs against their Turkish despots, and it is the peculiar glory of the Slavonic committees that they were able to give rapid effect to the enthusiasm kindled in Russia by the story of the sufferings of our brethren, and by sustaining the struggle for emancipation were able to keep the condition of the Slavs before the Powers until at last the Russian Government stepped in to free them from bondage. All Russia—Czar, Government, and all—is now but one vast Slavonic Committee for the liberation of the Southern Slavs; and we have far less reason for wishing to destroy a State which has so nobly undertaken the heroic task of liberating our brethren than Englishmen have for desiring to upset their Parliamentary system which has enabled a Lord Beaconsfield to balk the generous aspirations expressed by the nation during the autumn of 1876.

It is entirely false that to our Slav Committees belongs the honour of having originated the insurrection of the Herzegovina. After it began it attracted our attention, and we would have assisted it if we could, but, unfortunately, the Russian people were not aroused, and there were next to no funds at our disposal to assist the heroic insurgents whose desperate resolve to achieve liberty or death on their native hills first compelled the Powers to face what Europe calls the Eastern Question, but what we call the emancipation of the Slavs. The utmost that we could do in the first year of the insurrection was to collect some £10,000 for the relief of the refugees in the Herzegovina, Montenegro, and Ragusa. English sympathisers, notably Mr. Freeman, also collected contributions for the same cause. General Tchernayeff proposed in September to take fifty non-commissioned officers to Montenegro, with arms for five hundred men; but he could not carry out his scheme because we had no funds. I state this as a matter of fact, which I regret. It is the duty of free Slavs to assist their enslaved brethren to throw off the yoke of bondage. Our war may be condemned, but the heroism of our volunteers is appreciated even by those who support the Turks. Mr. Kinglake, for example—who, I regret to say, withholds from our cause the great influence of his illustrious name—refers to this aspect of the question in the Preface of the last edition of his "Crimean War," in terms so generous and yet so just, that no Russian can read his words without the deepest emotion. Can Englishmen wonder that we Russians, brethren in race and in religion to the Rayahs of Northern Turkey, should endeavour to assist them as the English of Elizabeth's reign endeavoured to assist the Protestants of Holland and of France? But the fact that we would glory in assisting our enslaved brethren to throw off the yoke of the Turk should entitle us to be believed when we sorrowfully admit that as a matter of fact we have no claim to the credit of having fomented the insurrection which every one now can see was a death-blow to the domination of the Ottoman. It was not till after the insurrection had made considerable progress—not, in fact, until the atrocities in Bulgaria and the Servian war—that Russia awoke and assumed the liberating mission which, after great and terrible sacrifices, promises at last to be crowned with complete success.

It is a mistake to say that our Russian volunteers in Servia were paid. It is also false that 9,000 Russians went to Servia. We could only find the travelling expenses of 4,000, none of whom received any other pay, but all of whom were willing—nay, joyful—to die for the cause. One-third of them perished as martyrs, but their blood has not been shed in vain. Their death sealed the doom of the Turks. The Czar has undertaken the championship of the Slavonic cause, and the war will only end when the liberation of the Southern Slavs is complete. So far from desiring the war to destroy the Czardom, we were never so proud of Russia as we are to-day; never were we so unanimously and enthusiastically united in support of our heroic Czar, who, after liberating twenty-three millions of serfs at home, is now crowning his reign with glory by emancipating the Southern Slavs.

LETTER II.

THE TWO RUSSIAS—MOSCOW AND ST. PETERSBURG.

LETTER II.

THE TWO RUSSIAS—MOSCOW AND ST. PETERSBURG.

[*The "Times" of Nov. 14, 1877, published a letter from its correspondent in St. Petersburg, describing a minority in the Russian capital as wearied of the war and anxious to make peace, regardless of the fate of the Southern Slavs. The "Pall Mall Gazette," noticing his remarks under the suggestive heading "Reported return of reason in Russia," exulted in the hope that the Russians were about to abandon their heroic enterprise. This delusion can be removed most effectually by the simple statement of facts, too often ignored in England.*]

"SO the people who made the war are already repenting of their folly!" sneers an exponent of the gospel of cynicism, as he lays down the *Times* of last Wednesday, after perusing a letter from its St. Petersburg correspondent with the above heading. "Indeed!" I exclaim, with unfeigned surprise, "that is strange news. Who says so? What is your authority?"

"The St. Petersburg correspondent of the *Times*," rejoins the cynic, "who, as the *Pall Mall Gazette* says, is known as the writer of a famous book on Russia, which appeared some months ago—in other words, all but naming Mr. R. Mackenzie Wallace."

"And Mr. Wallace says the people who made the war are repenting of what they did," I continue. "Where does he say so? I don't see any such statement in his letter."

"Do you not?" he asks in amazement. "What can be plainer than his account of the regret with which the war, its objects, and its sacrifices are spoken of in St. Petersburg by men who 'consider themselves good patriots.' Here, for instance, he speaks of the statesman or official dignitary, the representative of the St. Petersburg Liberal press, and the commercial man, all of whose sentiments are faithfully reproduced. What more would you have as a proof that those who made the war are repenting in sackcloth and ashes of their Quixotic undertaking?"

I could not help smiling. "And so that is the evidence upon which you and Mr. Wallace build your theories of 'peace possibilities in Russia!'

These people—they did not make the war! Not they, indeed! It was not these 'patriots' to whose voices our Emperor gave ear!"

And so dismissing my Turkophile acquaintance, let me in a few sentences correct the false impression which that letter in the *Times* has produced, as the high character and deserved reputation of its author may mislead many.

The English people were told last year, and truly told, that there are two Russias. There is official Russia, and national Russia. There is, in a word, the Russia of St. Petersburg, and the Russia of Moscow. Now, the *Times* correspondent lives in St. Petersburg, and he transmits faithfully enough to England his impressions of public opinion in St. Petersburg. The only danger is that his readers may mistake St. Petersburg for Russia. But St. Petersburg, thank God! is not Russia, any more than the West-end of London is England. The whole course of European history, for the last two years, would be utterly incomprehensible on the contrary hypothesis. It was because foreigners took their impression of Russia from St. Petersburg that they blundered so grossly about the course which events would take in the East, and they will blunder not less grossly if, disregarding the lessons of the past, they once more entertain the hollow fallacy that the national opinion of Russia can be ascertained in the *salons* of St. Petersburg or by interviewing official personages on the banks of the Neva.

There are good men and true in St. Petersburg, as there are good men and true even in the clubs of Pall Mall; but the typical St. Petersburger, of whom Mr. Wallace writes, is as destitute of faith and of enthusiasm as the West-ender. But just as you say London is Turkophile, although many Londoners are anti-Turks, so we say St. Petersburg is anti-Slav. But then it must not be forgotten that St. Petersburg is not Russia. Peter the Great styled it "a window out of which Russia could look upon the Western world;" but it is not a window by which the Western world can look in upon Russia. No, St. Petersburg is not Russian! It is cosmopolitan. It is not vitalised with the fierce warm current of Russia's life-blood. It stands apart. It undoubtedly exercises a great influence in ordinary times, but at great crises it is powerless. St. Petersburg did its best to avert the war. It sneered at our Servian volunteers—nay, if it had had its way it would have arrested them as malefactors. Those who went first to Servia on their heroic mission were compelled to smuggle themselves as it were out of the country for fear of the interference of officialdom supreme at St. Petersburg. St. Petersburg would, if it could, have suppressed our Slav Committees, and it did its best to induce our generous Czar to violate that knightly word which he pledged at Moscow, amid the unbounded enthusiasm of all his subjects, to take up the cause of the Slavs, "although he had to take it up alone." In the midst of the great uprising of the nation occasioned by the Bulgarian atrocities and the Servian war, St. Petersburg was comparatively unmoved,—a mere dead cold cinder in the midst of the glowing warmth of our national revival. All the diplomatic negotiations which preceded the war are inexplicable unless this is borne in mind. My countrymen, rising in the sacred wrath kindled by the inexpiable wrongs inflicted upon their kinsmen, pressed sternly, steadily onward to redress these wrongs, to terminate for ever the *status quo*, which rendered them chronic, inevitable. Official Russia, unable to arrest the movement entirely, nevertheless attempted, and attempted in vain, to divert it by diplomatic contrivances. We had one device after another invented in rapid succession to avoid the war by which alone our brethren could be freed. It is humiliating to recall the tortuous windings of Russian diplomacy, the inexhaustible expedients by which the Petersburg party endeavoured to balk the fulfilment of the national aspirations.

The last of these was the Protocol! By that famous document official Russia consented, for the sake of the European concert and the peace of the Continent, to postpone indefinitely all action on behalf of the Southern Slavs, receiving in return for this sacrifice of her mission a promise that the Great Powers would watch the Turks, and after a period of time, not particularly specified, when it had once more, for the thousandth time, been demonstrated to the satisfaction even of the diplomatic mind that Turkish domination is utterly incapable of reform, improvement, or other amelioration than its total destruction, the Powers promised—oh, great concession!—to consider what should then be done to save our tortured brethren from the Ottoman horde. This was the patent St. Petersburg device for disappointing the hopes of the Russian people, and eagerly these officials, representatives of the Liberal press, and commercial men, who are now prating of peace to the *Times* correspondent, hoped that it would stave off what they are deriding now as the "Quixotic enterprise" of the War of Liberation. In Moscow, however—that great heart of the Russian Empire—the suspense occasioned by the negotiations about the Protocol was one longdrawn-out agony. Those who lived in the very heart of the national movement can never forget the terrible forebodings of these dismal days. We all moved under the pressure of a great dread. Was it to end thus? Were all our sacrifices to be sacrificed; was the blood of our martyrs spilt in vain? Was Holy Russia Holy Russia no more, but a mere appanage to cosmopolitan St. Petersburg? When the news came that the English Cabinet was insisting upon alterations we breathed more freely. "Demobilisation!" we cried. "No, it is not demobilisation; it is demoralisation! The Czar is too noble, too good a Russian; he will never consent to that!" But, then, again the news came that even that was to be accepted; and the sky grew very dark overhead, and we went about as if in the chamber of death, speaking in low accents and oppressed by a terrible fear of that national dishonour which we Russians, strange as it may appear to some people, dread even more than death! At last, to our great relief, the cloud lifted, the darkness disappeared, for the Turks rejected the Protocol; and the declaration of war was as grateful to us as the bright burst of sunlight in the east after a long, dark, stormy night.

And here may I venture, as a Russian, to say that, for securing by his provisoes the rejection of the Protocol by the Turks, Lord Derby has at least done one good thing at the English Foreign Office. He may not have intended it, but, as a matter of fact, he was our most efficient ally. But for him St. Petersburg might have triumphed. Russia might have been disgraced, and the Turks might have received a new lease of power. The Slav world has reason to thank him for having secured the victory of our cause by rendering it impossible for Russia to refrain from drawing the sword in the cause of the Southern Slavs.

Even St. Petersburg could not shrink from the contest after that last deadly blow was administered by the Turks to the schemes of the diplomatists. The war began. It is going on, and it will go on until the end is accomplished. No babble of St. Petersburg will now be able to bring that war to a dishonourable close; and no peace can be honourable that does not secure the object of the war. St. Petersburg is even worse than usual just now. Its best elements are in Bulgaria and Roumania. The Czar is there, and the sight of the fiendish atrocities perpetrated by the Turks upon our patient soldiers can only confirm his resolution to persevere "until the end." And behind him there stands, arrayed as one man, the whole Russian nation, ready to endure any sacrifices rather than leave the Turk to re-establish his desolating sovereignty over our brethren.

Is it so strange to Englishmen that there should

be two Russias? Are there not two Englands? The England that is true to English love for liberty, and the England that sees in liberty itself only a text for a sneer? There is the England of St. James's Hall* and the England of the Guildhall. An England with a soul and a heart, and an England which has only a pocket. In other words, there is the England of Mr. Gladstone and the England of Lord Beaconsfield. We Russians, too, have our sordid cynics, but they are in a minority. They may sneer, but they cannot rule; and, with that distinction, let me conclude by saying that these Petersburg *Tchinovniks*, whose views Mr. Wallace reproduces, are now what they have always been, the Beaconsfields of Russia!

' * I desire to remind the friends of the poor Slavs of the debt of gratitude they owe to the Eastern Question Association for its successful efforts to disseminate sound information on the subject of the war. The foreign readers will be glad to know that the above Association originated in the St. James's Hall Conference. The Duke of Westminster and the Earl of Shaftesbury are respectively President and Vice-President; Mr. William Morris, Treasurer; Messrs. G. Howard, F. W. Chesson, and J. W. Probyn, Hon. Secretaries; and Mr. E. S. Pryce, Secretary. The offices are in Great George Street, Westminster.

LETTER III.

COMPENSATION FOR SACRIFICES.

LETTER III.

COMPENSATION FOR SACRIFICES.

[*Prince Wassiltchikoff, President of the Slavonic Committee at St. Petersburg, published in the "Sévernoy Vestnik" an article on the compensation which in his own private opinion Russia had a right to demand at the end of the war; the importance ascribed to his suggestions in England called forth the following letter.*]

"IT is utterly impossible," said a friend of mine, "to make Englishmen believe that any nation is capable of doing anything from unselfish motives. If you tell them so they think at once that you are humbugging them!"

"Could you not persuade them that it is possible for a nation to go mad?" I asked.

"Yes," said he; "in that case it is possible that they may believe you—not otherwise!"

Well, I thought, if to perform an act of heroic

self-sacrifice is to be mad, the Russian nation is mad,—and I am proud of it! This is undoubtedly a mad war, if it is viewed as a speculation. It is evidently either a folly or a heroism!

"Do you believe that Russia is levying an unselfish war?" I have been asked incredulously, "Is it for the Southern Slavs she is fighting? Not for Kars, Batoum, and the free passage of the Dardanelles?"

"Answer me," I replied. "You English are great financiers. Will the war pay as a speculation? What possible compensation would repay us for our losses? Will the killed come to life again, or would we feel their death less keenly if we annexed Armenia?"

"No," he objected, "but Governments pay scant heed to the agonies inflicted upon the tools of their ambition."

"The Government, then; is it a good speculation for it? How much is the war costing us? We have lost 70,000 men already, and every man, your economists say, has a money value. The campaign is costing about £250,000 per day, or more. Take the smaller sum, and ask yourself whether all the territory which we can possibly gain is worth the cost?"

"Why, then," he rejoined, "do you go on fighting—for prestige?"

"Listen," I said; 'your child is attacked by a wolf. At the peril of your life you rush to the rescue, and kill the animal. What would you feel if a neighbour asked with a sneer why you could take so much trouble when the skin of a wolf is worth so little? It is our duty, and duty is the first of 'Russian interests.' As for prestige, there are moments in national, as in private, life when such trivial considerations are out of the question."

Apropos of compensation, Prince Wassiltchikoff's article in the *Sévernoy Vestnick* deals with that very subject. The word is badly chosen. There can be no compensation for sacrifices such as ours but the complete deliverance of the Slavs. Prince Wassiltchikoff fears that in a moment of impulsive magnanimity we may refuse all compensation for the labours and the blood which the war has cost us. Compensation is impossible. He demands a war fine as a matter of duty. But what fine can we exact from the bankrupt Ottoman?

Prince Wassiltchikoff, who, however, speaks solely in his own name, suggests that, not being able to pay in cash, the Turk might surrender his fleet. The suggestion has created some little stir—perhaps needlessly. Before the war is over not only the fleet, but even Turkey in Europe, may have ceased to exist. As the *Moscow Gazette* graphically remarked—" When a man dies the soul disappears, but the body remains. With the Russian navy the case is reversed. In the Black Sea the fleet exists no more; but its spirit survives to animate our heroic sailors, whose torpedoes have already diminished the number of Turkish ironclads." The gallantry of Dubassoff, Shistakoff, Prince Galitzine, and many others, encourages the hope that other men-of-war may share the fate of the monitors sunk in the Matchin Canal.

Prince Wassiltchikoff's innocent suggestion has raised quite a little storm in the English papers. "This is Russia's magnanimity," cry the Turkophiles. " Her crusade of emancipation was a mere pretext to cover her design on Turkish ironclads !"

Remarks of this kind could easily be foreseen. But Turkish ironclads are not the best representatives of European fleets.* Many of them are already out of repair, and they are getting worse daily. There are not twenty-five of them altogether. Yet Russia, if disengaged now, would be purchasing them at two millions per ship. A pretty bargain, is it not? Let us stick to our arithmetic. Russia, they say, has gone to war on the chance of gaining the Turkish fleet. Well, let us see what Russia is paying for her bargain. The war will not cost a penny less than £50,000,000. How much more money will be spent before we can demand the fleet as an indemnity is unknown. But the Turkish navy, even when new, surely did not cost so much. What does a sea-going ironclad of the latest fashion cost? About half a million—is it not so? Then with the money

* Since the above was written I am glad to find my observations confirmed by no less an authority than Lord Eustace Cecil, Under Secretary of the English War Office, whose Turkish sympathies are undisguised. Speaking at Hereford on December 1st, he said that the Turkish fleet, having been built at least a dozen years ago, as a power of offence was almost useless, for its armour plates were only constructed to resist guns of a very inferior calibre. He did not believe there was one Turkish ironclad that would resist either a 38 or a 35-ton gun.

spent already we could have bought a hundred first-class ironclads. I am not quick at figures, but that is simple enough. The Turks have not even ten first-class vessels. But, then, say the timid Englishmen who are always pretending to be afraid of Russia, it is the sudden increase of Russian naval power that is the danger we dread. You might have bought a better fleet, but not all at once. It would need four or five years. Well, suppose it would! But do you think that, after such a tremendous war as the present, we shall be anxious—even if we were ever so aggressive—to attack any one else for at least that time? We would need longer to heal our wounds and to repair our losses; and in that time England and the other Powers could proportionately increase their navies.

Germany took five milliards from France without English objections. If we could take half of that sum from the Turks England probably would not object neither. But, with one quarter of that money, we could build twice as good a fleet as the Turks have now, and have it ready—with the assistance of the English and American

Compensation for Sacrifices.

ship-builders—as soon as we could possibly be in a position to use the Turkish fleet, if it passed into our hands.

If we got the Turkish fleet, who knows but that we might sell it in order to pay part—a very small part—of our war expenses?

The *Times*, I see, suggests that after we Russians have beaten the Turks the fleet should be sold by auction for the benefit of the Turkish bondholders! How very kind and considerate in the *Times*! I do enjoy that proposal! We Russians have such strong reasons for sympathising with the English holders of Ottoman bonds! But for them and the money which they poured into the pocket of the Sultan this war would long since have been over. Every thousand pounds lent to the Turk by England has cost Russia perhaps more than one precious life. Should the fleet of the Turk ever come into our hands we certainly shall not use it to raise money for the distressed bondholders. Better burn it! But the suggestion is probably only *une mauvaise plaisanterie*—a bad little joke on the part of the *Times*.

Yet I hear the City people accept the suggestion

as a very happy one, and almost fancy that it will greatly delight Turkey if her navy becomes the prey of her generous protector. It seems to me, however, that, although the Turks have had plenty of words of sympathy and promises of help from England, they have little cause for gratitude for so platonic a devotion, which only had the effect of irritating Russia. The worst friends of the Turks, from the first, have been those men who are now speaking as if they had deserved the fleet as a reward for counsels which lured their friends to ruin.

Prince Wassiltchikoff is a man of high character and position. I never met anybody who did not esteem the straightforwardness of his views; but with all that I fail to understand why the *Times* should treat his theory about the Dardanelles question as if his letter were written by Prince Gortschakoff.* Russians are not sent to Siberia for having an opinion of their own about affairs in the East. Prince Gortschakoff, in his despatch to

* It turns out that the Prince never put forward as his own the view imputed to him, but introduced it for the purpose of refutation. It is to the credit of the *Manchester Guardian* that it discovered the blunder before the appearance of the authorized contradiction.

Compensation for Sacrifices.

Lord Derby, in May, expressly disclaimed any intention of settling the Dardanelles question, except in accordance with the views of the Powers of Europe. Of course our Imperial Chancellor knows all about these things better than I do; but I express an opinion, shared by many of my countrymen, that, in giving so many assurances, and making so many concessions to the Powers, Russia displays too great a condescension. Europe does not help us in our battle. Why should she interfere with the fruits of our victory?

LETTER IV.

TERMS OF PEACE—POSSIBLE AND IMPOSSIBLE.

LETTER IV.

TERMS OF PEACE—POSSIBLE AND IMPOSSIBLE.

Prince Gortschakoff, in his despatch to Lord Derby, dated May 18th, 1877, wrote as follows:—"As far as concerns Constantinople, without being able to prejudge the course or issue of the war, the Imperial Cabinet repeats that the acquisition of that capital is excluded from the views of His Majesty the Emperor. They recognise that in any case the future of Constantinople is a question of common interest, which cannot be settled otherwise than by a general understanding, and that if the possession of the city were to be put in question, it could not be allowed to belong to any of the European Powers." The Emperor had previously held similar language to Lord A. Loftus. No other introduction is necessary to the following letter.]

RUSSIAN papers mention a great personage who, on overhearing some discussion about the possible conclusion of peace, observed significantly that the time was too serious for jokes. Whoever the personage may be, we may bless him for his remark. Yet English people discuss the possibilities of peace without any consciousness that their talk cannot be regarded as serious. There is evidently an insurmountable difficulty on the part of Englishmen to understand the way in which we regard this war in Russia. Were it not so we should hear less of the hopes so freely expressed and so thoughtlessly cheered that foreign advice might guide Russia in bringing our war to a close. In England you have evidently forgotten all about the object of the war in the eagerness with which you have followed its details. The death-struggle in Bulgaria and Armenia is to you what a gladiatorial combat was to the pampered populace of ancient Rome. You sit as spectators round the arena, cheering now the Turk and now the Russian, as if these brave men were being butchered solely to afford you an exciting spectacle. Tired at last, you cry, "Enough, enough! clear the ring, and pass on to some other sport." But had you not ignored the nature of the fight you would never ask to do that. It is not a mere gladiator's war.

Terms of Peace—Possible and Impossible. 57

It is not a duel between two Powers about some punctilio of offended honour, which might be satisfied—as Mr. Freeman so well says—by the killing of a decent number of people. Were it either of these things there would be some reason for the tragedy to close, for it would have been a crime from the first. But the war in which my countrymen are dying by thousands, so far from being a crime was an imperative duty, for it was the only means for attaining an end the righteousness of which all Europe has admitted. It was the only way for Russia of being consistent.

We did not make war for the sake of war. We sorrowfully but resolutely accepted that terrible alternative because we had no other choice, since ill-advised Turkey would not listen to the voice of justice. To us it would be a crime if, after having begun the work, we were to draw back without having accomplished the object which alone justified so terrible an undertaking. Hence all this talk of mediation, intervention, conferences, and of peace proposals sounds to us as mere mockery. There can be no peace until we have attained our end, and that we cannot do until we have completely freed the Christian Slavs. The war to us is a cruel reality, instead of merely a theatrical spectacle, We bear the blows the mere sight of which unnerves you. It is our hearths that are darkened by the shadow of death. Yet in all Russia you will hear no cry for peace until we have secured our end. I grieve to say Russia has its Beaconsfields. But as I said before, they are in a minority, and they become what they ought to be — thoroughly Russian, when asked to die for their country. Amongst the heroes whose deaths Russia deplores were people who—thanks to foreign influences. thanks to an idle, unoccupied life—became estranged from national interests; but their hearts throbbed afresh on hearing cries for help in accents of agony, and on seeing with their own eyes the appalling miseries of their brethren. The war brings out to daylight the best, the noblest elements of my country. Our armies are appreciated by the whole world. Colonel Brackenbury's eloquent tribute to the Russian character, published by the *Times* (December 1st), carries with it such a strong conviction of its absolute accuracy that it cannot be read without producing feelings of sympathy and admiration. As a Russian I read and re-read it with deep emotions of gratitude. There is another side of the question, which, although seldom mentioned by the press, deserves the highest praise—I mean the part played in the war by the Russian women. From the highest to the lowest rank, regardless of any social differences, they devote themselves entirely to the relief of the sick and wounded, both on the field of battle and at home. In fact, the Red Cross Society includes in its ranks the whole womanhood of Russia. This spirit of self-sacrifice and devotion is shown even by those who, before the testing moment, appeared to be utterly lost in worldly, frivolous pursuits.

Yes, this grand war has given a new impulse to Russian life, a deeper feeling of higher missions in this world. Someone said that life was nothing but an examination one had to pass in order to die nobly, and to prove that we did not make a bad use of the greatest privilege given to mortals —that of moral liberty. My countrymen and countrywomen are passing their examination splendidly; and the Slavs — the cause of this new heroism of the whole of Russia — have claims upon our gratitude as much as upon our sympathies! If it had not been for Servia and the Russian volunteers there, the Slavonic world might have waited for its deliverance many, many years more.

In vain we try to pierce the impervious veil which conceals the future, but we know that our Czar is the very incarnation of his country, and that having often shown a remarkable kindheartedness, he has also given striking proofs of his firm will in great, decisive moments. The fate of the Christian Slavs is in noble and generous hands. The result of the war no Russian can for one moment doubt. Come what may, the Slavs will be freed. All "possible terms of peace," that do not include the ejection of the Zaptieh and the Pasha, bag and baggage, from the Balkans are manifestly impossible. Deluded and obstinate as the Turk is, he will not go out until he is beaten *à plates coutures*.

After the barbarian is swept away the task of reorganising the Government of these lands will be much simplified. It will not be impossible to maintain sufficient order in the province while its

Terms of Peace—Possible and Impossible. 61

inhabitants are gradually acquiring, like the Serbs and Roumans, the habit of self-government. As to Constantinople, even if the fortune of war should compel us to enter that city, we should enter it as the Germans entered Paris, to celebrate a triumph, not to make an annexation. Our Emperor's word upon this was solemn and conclusive.

The refusal to believe such an assurance from such a man implies an incapacity to understand the very existence of good faith. Only souls darkened by their own deceit are blind to the rays which stream from the sun of truth. Certain suspicions reflect discredit only upon those who entertain them. The nobler England is above such unworthy distrust.

Roumania stretches as a barrier between us and the soil of Turkey which we are supposed to covet, and Roumania will not suffer for her alliance with Russia. We have no warmer allies than the foremost statesmen and scholars of England. Only two or three days ago Sir George Cox, the eminent historian of Greece, urged his countrymen to present an address to the Czar assuring him that in the great work of freeing Europe wholly and for ever from the defilement of Turkish rule we heartily wish him and all his people "God speed," and that we wait impatiently for the day when the Russian Emperor shall proclaim the freedom of the Christian subjects of the Sultan in the city of Constantine. There only can the work be consummated; and there, by establishing European law, and then withdrawing from the land which he shall have set free, he will have won for himself an undying glory, and, what is of infinitely greater moment, he will have done his duty in the sight of God and man.

Well, it is a difficult question! The *Guardian*, I see, advises us to annex Armenia. Mr Forster and Mr Bryce declared that for the Armenians Russian annexation would be a great change for the better. They received our troops as deliverers, and thousands accompanied them on their retreat into Russian territory. We cannot surrender these poor creatures into the hands of the Turks. What must we do, then? If we retire the Turk will return, and the last state of Armenia will be worse than the first. Russia is wealthy enough in territory, but what are we to do about the Armenians? This difficulty is not felt by Russians alone, but is shared by Englishmen who have studied the question. One of those whose name stands high in the literary world, remarked, the other day:—

"You have captured Kars thrice this century. Why should you give it up? The Germans did not give up Metz. They did not desire any conquest, they aimed at no aggrandisement; but they kept Metz as a safeguard against another war. Suppose you keep Kars, who has any right to complain? Not the Turks, for the victor has a right to the spoils. As for the other Powers, if they had helped you in your battle they might have claimed to be heard, but not now."

Then there is Batoum. It is close on our frontier. It is notorious that it is solely due to a misspelling in an old treaty that it is not already ours. Why should we not rectify the clerical mistake of the transcriber? Batoum is the natural port of Russian Armenia. Its harbour is most frequented by Russian ships. It was certainly not worth while going to war for Batoum or Kars, and the Turkish fleet into the bargain. But now that we have had to go to war, is it not a moral duty to make the Turks pay as dearly as possible for the sacrifices which they have cost us? If we could punish the Turks without annexing any territory I would not annex either Kars or Batoum; but if that is the only way in which they can be punished, and the Armenians protected, my scruples against annexation may disappear.

There were many of us in Russia when war was declared who believed that the whole of the campaign would be simply a military promenade. Many said, "We will occupy Constantinople in June or July, and, after dictating in that capital our terms of peace, we will return home with the happy consciousness that we have arranged everything to our satisfaction." But now we are in November; we have lost 71,000 men killed and wounded; we are spending millions and millions for the war, and we are not yet in occupation of Constantinople. The difficulty and costliness of the enterprise render it impossible for Russia to secure any adequate compensation for her sacrifices. We may get some kind of an indemnity—using the word to signify a war fine,—and it is well to distinguish between a war fine and compensation. We have made great sacrifices, and we may yet have to make still greater should Lord Beaconsfield succeed in arraying England against us; but the liberation of the Slavs is now certain. Between the *status quo ante bellum* and the present lie too many precious graves for it ever to be restored. Our military promenade has transformed itself into a gigantic burial procession; but when its end is attained our regret for the brave who have fallen in the fight will be rendered less poignant by the joy with which we shall hail the resurrection of the Southern Slavs.

LETTER V.

WHY RUSSIANS HATE THE TURKS.

LETTER V.

WHY RUSSIANS HATE THE TURKS.

WHY do the Russians hate the Turks?
Because they know them.

An all-sufficient answer. Our knowledge was not bought without bitter tears. The Tartar wrote his character across our Russia in letters of flame. You English people are not touched with a feeling of the sufferings of the rayahs because you have not been in all points afflicted as they. Russians have. In centuries of anguish they have learned the lesson of sympathy with those who are crushed beneath an Asiatic yoke. We feel for them because we suffered with them. As they are—so we were. They are not only our brethren in race and religion, they are also our brothers in misfortune, united to us in "the sacred communion of sorrow."

Many of my English friends know but little about the causes of hereditary hatred of the Russian for the Turk. I venture, therefore, to state briefly the facts which my countrymen can never forget.

It is more than six hundred years since first the Russian people fell under the curse of Tartar domination. Before that time the Russians were as free, as prosperous, and as progressive as their neighbours. Serfdom was unknown. The knout, Mr. Tennyson's abomination, was not introduced until two hundred and fifty years after the Tartar conquest. There were Republics in Russia as in Italy, and the Grand Prince had no more power than other sovereigns. But in the middle of the thirteenth century Russia, lying nearest to Asia, experienced a Tartar invasion. An accident of geographical position subjected her to a visitation, from the consequences of which she has freed herself by superhuman struggles.

It was in 1224 that the Tartars first established themselves as conquerors in South-Eastern Russia. It was not till the close of the sixteenth century that we finally rid ourselves of these troublesome intruders. The Tartar domination, however, did not last much more than two hundred years. It was in 1252 that St. Alexander Nevsky received the title of Grand Duke from the Tartars. It was not till 1476 that we ceased to pay tribute to our conquerors. But long after Ivan III. had broken the power of the Mongol horde the Tartars spread desolation and death through Russia. As late as 1571, when England, under Elizabeth, had just given birth to a Shakespeare, Moscow was burnt to the ground by a wandering host of Asiatics.

It is easy to write the words, "invaded by the Tartars;" but who can realize the "fact"? Western Europe, which felt afar off the scorching of the storm of fire which swept over Russia, throbbed with horror. Kind-hearted St. Louis of France prayed "that the Tartars might be banished to the Tartarus from whence they had come, lest they might depopulate the earth." All the monsters who to you are mere names were to us horrible realities. The Khans, the Begs, whose pyramids of skulls the world still hears with dread, rioted in rapine throughout the whole of Russia. Five generations of Russians lived and died under the same degrading yoke as that which has crushed the manhood out of the Bulgarians.

For centuries every strolling Tartar was as absolute master of the life, the property, and the honour of Russians as the Zaptieh is of the lives of the Southern Slavs. To you English people atrocities are things to read of and imagine. To us Russians they are a repetition of horrors with which we have been familiar from childhood. Moscow has twice suffered the fate of Batak, and nearly every city in Russia has suffered the horrors inflicted upon Yeni-Zagra.

For at least three centuries our national history is little more than a record of the struggle of our race for liberty to live. Our national heroes are the warriors who did battle with the Asiatic intruder, and to this hour in our churches the images of St. Alexander Nevsky fighting the Tartars stir the patriotism and excite the imagination of the youthful Russian. The path of liberty was steep and thorny. Again and again our efforts were baffled. A town revolted, and it was consumed. Bands of armed peasants who resisted the Tartars were from time to time massacred to a man. But the Russian nation did not despair. As your own Byron sang—Byron, who gave his life to the cause for which thousands of my countrymen are giving theirs to-day—

> "Freedom's battle, once begun,
> Bequeathed by bleeding sire to son,
> Though baffled oft, is ever won."

Gradually Russia shook off the yoke of her oppressors. Her advance resembled that of Servia and Roumania. After having enjoyed administrative autonomy she secured her position as a tributary State, and then at last, waxing strong with freedom, she burst the chains with which she had been so long bound.

Russia was free from the Asiatic oppressor, but the evil results of his domination remained. Mr. Gladstone, in one of his grandest speeches on the Eastern Question, explained the comparatively low intellectual condition of the Southern Slavs by referring to the sandy barrier which, while producing nothing valuable itself, nevertheless keeps the destroying wave from encroaching upon the fertile land. What the Southern Slavs did South

Russia did for Northern Europe. Upon us the Asiatic wave spent its force. We were overwhelmed. But we saved Europe from the Mongol horde.

While we saved we suffered; we emerged from the flood of barbarism ourselves partially barbarous. Our progress had been arrested for centuries. All our national energies had been diverted into the struggle against our conquerors. What had once been flourishing towns were blackened ruins. Liberty itself disappeared for a time. To fight the Tartar all power was centred in the hand of one ruler. Serfdom was amongst the legacies of Tartar domination. While the rest of the world had advanced, Russia had even been forced back.

It was a terrible visitation, but it left behind it at least one benefit. But for the tortures of these sad centuries, the Russian people might have been as indifferent as the French and the English to the cries of those who are still under the power of the Pashas. But for the sympathy of the Russian people Chefket Pasha and Achmet Aga might have ruled for ever in Bosnia and Bulgaria. The Tartars prevented that. They taught the Russian people what the rule of the Asiatic is,—a dreadful lesson, creating that inextinguishable hatred of the Turk which will ultimately secure his ejection from Europe. The death-warrant of the Ottoman was signed by Timour the Tartar.

LETTER VI.

SOME ENGLISH PREJUDICES.

LETTER VI.

SOME ENGLISH PREJUDICES.

ALAS! poor Russians! we seem to have no chance, no chance whatever, of obtaining justice among the English in England. No sooner do we flatter ourselves that at last we have met with a friend—with at least one person who has the courage not to accept as gospel all that is alleged against us without positive evidence, not to regard separate cases as general absolute truths—than a rude rebuff recalls us to the region of unpleasant but actual fact, and an act of pure unmistakeable hostility dissipates in a moment the pleasing illusion that at last we had found someone to understand us. Why is it that so many English people hate us? There must be some strange subtle antipathy which baffles analysis, just as there is an equally strange sympathy which wins for the Turk, in spite of his revolting misdeeds, the affection of Englishmen.

Why can it be? Fear can surely have no share in the production of so persistent an animosity, so inveterate a prejudice! The menace to your Indian realm exists only in the imagination of those who fancy that it is but a stone's throw from the banks of the Oxus to the southern slopes of the Himalayas. In Russia we cannot understand why Englishmen should pay us the exaggerated compliment of permitting a dread of Russian power to colour all the speeches of your Conservative politicians, and to bias the policy of your Ministry. We know too much of the power of England to accept such a compliment as quite *au serieux*. It is to us just a little too absurd. We see that England annexes new territories every year with a facility which betrays to foreigners little evidence of reluctance on her part to extend the boundaries of her Empire. We know that she is all-powerful at sea, and able to command everything that money can procure on the land at a moment's notice. Russia, on the other hand, is not wealthy. She is only morally rich in the consciousness that she is performing her duty, and moral wealth according to old-fashioned Russian views is not altogether to be despised. But that moral wealth can neither threaten India nor annex Great Britain. Why, then, this irrational panic, which haunts the imagination of what used to be the most self-confident, self-reliant, and fearless race in the world? If I were an Englishman I should blush for shame if I entertained the coward fear of any Power on earth.

It is impossible to believe that fears so groundless can really occasion all the hostility with which my country is regarded by many Englishmen. If it is not fear, to what unknown source, then, can we trace the origin of Russophobia? To poor simple-minded Russians it may seem a hopeless task to undertake such an inquiry. As incomprehensible in its origin as it is illogical in its manifestation, they are content to dismiss it with that phrase which has served as a refuge to so many baffled inquirers—"There are more things in heaven and earth, Horatio, than are dreamt of in your philosophy." But perhaps I may be pardoned if I suggest that ignorance, pure, sheer, downright ignorance, has not a little to do with it.

Let me give an instance of this ignorance in places where it might least be expected to exist. The other day a friend mentioned, in the course of conversation, that your great English poet, Mr. Tennyson, hated Russia.

"Indeed," said I; "that is most unfortunate. But can you tell me why?"

"Oh," was the response, "we English people, you know, cannot tolerate your knout system!"

"How good of you!" I exclaimed; "upon this we perfectly agree. But tell me, why should your Laureate live only in the past and take no notice of the present? Poets are not confined to the contemplation of the past; the future itself is sometimes disclosed to their ken."

With a puzzled look and hesitating accent, he observed, "But you do not mean to say that the knout is a thing of the past, not of the present?"

"That is exactly what I do mean to say," I answered. "If I wish to stick to facts I can say nothing else. The knout has ceased to exist in Russia. Even in the navy," I added, "which perhaps is also the case with the cat-o'-nine-tails in the navy of England! Is it not so?"

Without answering my question, my friend said, "Since when?"

"Shortly after the emancipation of the serfs," said I. "Russia is a long way off; but is fifteen years not long enough for such a reform to reach the ears of England's Laureate?"

We may be "barbarians," but our criminal code, judged by the standard of the Howard Association, is more humane than that of at least one other nation which retains the lash in the marine, applies the cat-o'-nine-tails to the garotter, and secretly strangles murderers in the recesses of her gaols.

Well, perhaps that does not improve matters. Is ignorance not invincible? Does not Schiller say "against stupidity the gods themselves contend in vain"? If Englishmen, fifteen years after the knout has disappeared from Russia, persist in denouncing Russians for using the knout, what can we hope? And here again we Russians labour at a great disadvantage. We shrink from the task of vindicating ourselves even from the most unjust reproaches. Some accusations appear to us so inconceivably absurd that we cannot understand how any answer can be required.

Let me illustrate this. Last year a curious collection of calumnies against Russia was anonymously published in England. My English friends, to whose judgment I attach the greatest importance, were anxious that it should be refuted. I applied, and applied in vain, to one after another of my literary friends in Russia to undertake such a task. "How can you ask such a thing! No Russian with any self-respect could stoop to notice such monstrous libels. Your beloved England is evidently demoralising you, or you would never pay attention to such attacks." Is it either right or generous to declare that because no reply is made no reply can be made? The *Golos* last year published a long and circumstantial story of the way in which Lord Beaconsfield abused his position as Premier to influence the Money Market. Nobody in England dreamed of categorically refuting it. They regarded the calumny as beneath contempt. Has not a Russian as much right to silence when accused as Lord Beaconsfield?

I am the more disposed to attribute this strange antipathy to ignorance, because those Englishmen who really know us are among the best friends we have. If there were really some secret antipathy between the nations this would not be so. In cases of mutual repulsion the repulsion is most marked when the two objects approach. But English residents in Russia rarely manifest irrational antipathy which is so strongly shown on the banks of the Thames.

Examples of an exactly opposite feeling are present to our memory—such, for instance, as the warm-hearted letters which appeared in the *Daily News* and the *Times* last year, from well known English residents in Moscow; and, frankly speaking, I think they are only paying us with our own coin. Although the English Turkophile press delights to represent us as evil spirits, Russians who come to England are so kindly treated that they always want to come again.

I am aware that the mistake is often made of attaching too much importance to what is said in certain clubs or coteries in London, or by journals which notoriously speak under official or foreign influences. I have lived long enough in England to discover that public opinion is a force which may exist independently of the political society of the capital, or of a particular political party in the country. It is certain that among large classes of the English people—in Birmingham, Manchester, Edinburgh, and other great centres —there is a wide-spread conviction that Turkish misgovernment must no longer be supported by British bayonets; and that Russia is entitled to the moral sympathy of mankind in her efforts to liberate the oppressed Christians. While journals like the *Times,* the *Daily News,* the *Echo,* the *Spectator,* and the *Examiner* (many others might be mentioned) show that in London a strong feeling exists in favour of acting fairly to Russia, in the provinces and in Scotland the most widely circulated journals have resolutely opposed the Beaconsfield policy.*

The evidence of war correspondents of the

---

* I am anxious to mention the fact that the *Northern Echo* of Darlington is greatly appreciated and admired in Russia for the energetic, constant sympathy it has shown to the Slavonic cause. Long passages from its leading articles have been quoted both by M. Katkoff's *Moscow Gazette* and M. Guilaroft's *Contemporary News.* The above-mentioned gentlemen are proprietors and editors at the same time, as is almost always the case in Russian newspapers.

English press is not without some little weight Colonel Brackenbury, Mr. M'Gahan, Mr. Forbes, Sir Henry Havelock, Mr. Boyle, and others, less well-known, made the acquaintance of Russians in Roumania and Bulgaria under circumstances which render concealment of realities impossible. I desire no better verdict for my countrymen than that pronounced by those witnesses selected at random, although some were hostile and others did not spare their reproaches against what they believed to be wrong—for, after all, we cannot be vexed with people, although they do not arrive at exactly the right result, if they honestly do their best.

After the knout, Russia is most abused for her treatment of her subject races, and with as little reason. We have, for instance, many Mohammedan subjects. They are not oppressed, or persecuted. They have all the liberty enjoyed by the Mohammedans in Turkey, except the liberty of oppressing their Christian neighbours They certainly enjoy a far better Government than their co-religionists in Asia Minor. In the Baltic Provinces there are many local municipal institutions; and no race has less reason to complain of ill-treatment than the Germans, who enjoy so large a share of the administration of the Empire. It is a characteristic of Russia that we open even the highest branches of our service to all our subject races—an example which England, I think, does not follow in India. General Melikoff and General Lazareff, who have covered themselves with glory in Armenia, are both Armenians. Todleben and Heimann are Germans of the Baltic Provinces. Nepokoitschitzky is a Pole, as also is Levitsky.

"Ah, Poland!" you exclaim. Of course it is in vain for a Russian to appeal for a hearing of his defence about the Poles, even to those who deny Home Rule to the Irish. Sometime I may say something of Russian rule in Poland, but I content myself with saying that Poland would have had a Constitution of its own for the last fourteen years if the Poles would have been content with the boundaries of the kingdom of Poland. But when they insisted, even at the sword's point, that we should give Home Rule not only to Poland but almost to half Russia, which they claimed to be theirs, then a reaction set in, and the reforms which the Grand Duke Constantine went to Warsaw with such high hopes to establish remained a dead letter.

Constitutions are not unknown in Russia, nor is it beyond the boundaries of Russian policy to grant Home Rule to its subject provinces. Those who think so should go to Finland. In that important maritime province they would find the Finns in possession of a very large measure of administrative independence. The Russian language is not employed in Finnish Courts or in Finnish official documents. The Lutheran, and not the Russian Orthodox Church, is the established religion of Finland. Nay, even the Russian rouble will not circulate in that Russian province —which lies almost at the gates of the Russian capital. Finland has its own laws, its own legislature, its own Church, its own coinage, its own language, its own budget, and its own national debt.

Nor does the recognition of local independence destroy the loyalty of our Finns. During this war their enthusiasm has been very great, although they are connected neither by race nor religion with the Southern Slavs. There is no conscription in Finland. Its system of raising soldiers is the same as the English. A few weeks ago a call was made for volunteers in one district in Finland. In three days the list was more than filled by gallant men who were eager to be led to the liberation of Bulgaria. That they knew it was no holiday work upon which they had entered was shown by one grim little fact. Every volunteer before joining the ranks provided himself with a dagger, in order that he might have the means of saving himself by a swift death-stroke from the mutilation and torture that awaits the wounded who fall into the hands of the Turks! Have we not reason to be proud of men who go out joyfully to risk their lives in such a war?

It is difficult to convince those who are not familiar with Russia how willingly the whole population of my country will surrender all that they have, even life itself if it be required by the Czar, in order to carry on the war which he has undertaken for the oppressed Slavs. The declaration in the petitions which flowed in to the Czar after the Moscow address—"We place our fortunes and our

Some English Prejudices. 91

lives at thy disposal"—was no meaningless phrase. The records of Russia's history prove that it is a simple statement of a fact.

The calculating, sceptical, selfish part of Europe may look upon the addresses and petitions to the Czar merely as a species of new-fashioned eloquence. But in burning, decisive, historical moments such Russian words have always been synonymous with deeds. An offer of "life and fortune" can only be voluntary. We Russians are sometimes prevented from having this will categorically expressed and carried out; but after we have almost implored to be allowed to sacrifice them in a holy cause we never fear to be taken at our word—we never shrink from its consequences. The mighty voice of the Russian people has never been heard in vain.

Permit me to recall one instance alone out of numbers which might be mentioned to illustrate this characteristic of my countrymen. In the time of Peter the Great, whilst Russia was fighting, not for the tortured Slavs, not for her persecuted co-religionists, but merely for the possession of the Baltic Provinces—a question of comparatively small moment to the Russian people—the Czar sent an ukase to the Senate fixing new taxes upon salt. No sooner was the Imperial decree read than Prince Jacob Dolgorouky sprang from his chair, and in the presence of a numerous assemblage, to the bewilderment of everyone, tore it to pieces.

"Emperor!" exclaimed he, with a trembling voice, "you want money? We understand it! But why should the poor suffer and pay for it? Have you no wealthy nobility to dispose of? Prince Menshikoff may build a ship at his private expense, Apraxine another one, and I will certainly not remain behind my countrymen!"

Such was the spirit displayed by the Russians in those days, and since the time of Peter the Great Russians have not degenerated.

LETTER VII.

TRADITIONAL POLICY.

LETTER VII.

TRADITIONAL POLICY.

"WE must support the Turk, for it is our traditional policy," is the motto of England. No, not of England, but of many Englishmen The tradition, however, does not go very far back —not much farther, in fact, than the Crimean war—a war, the wisdom of which many of its authors now seriously doubt.

But I will not raise that question now. Grant it if you will that the Pasha and the Bashi-Bazouk are the traditional allies of free England. Must what has been always continue? Must the past bind for ever both the present and the future? The history of every nation is nothing but the changes in its traditional, internal, and external policy.

This persistency in the "traditional policy" reminds one of an incident in the reforming labours of Peter the Great. The genuine Russians, in his time, believed firmly in the wisdom of their ancestors. They walked in the old ways. The new was to them the profane. The old was holy. The reformer was the blasphemer, and few incidents in our history are more interesting than the attempt of the great Czar to civilize his subjects.

This task was almost too great, even for such a Titan as he. The inert conservatism of the masses would have baffled the strength of a Hercules. It was only by main force that he could compel his unwilling subjects to forsake the old ruts. Before he came to the throne, Archangel, far away in the frozen sea, was Russia's only port. Peter, with his ready sword, hewed his way to the Baltic, and the sea was gained. St. Petersburg was founded. But nothing was sent for shipment. The traders, disdaining to turn aside at St. Petersburg, continued to send their goods for shipment to Archangel. It was the traditional policy of their ancestors.

The Czar remonstrated with his subject-merchants. But as they had always gone to Archangel, they would always go to Archangel. Upon this Peter issued his positive order that the port should be closed altogether, and only by that means the trade took the nearer route. The past is full of illustrations of the necessity for deviating from the old lines of established custom, but the above incident is curious because it is an instance of a literal adhesion to an old road. It has many counterparts in politics. For instance, the change in England's traditional policy was effected by the forcible interference of a "Czar Peter" in the shape of the autumn agitation of 1876, but for which England might now have been at war with us against the cause of freedom in the East.

Policies must be adjusted to facts, not facts to policies. No rule of conduct can be immutable. The wisdom of yesterday is often the folly of to-day. To be truly consistent as to one's object, one must often be completely inconsistent as to the means.

The truth is not a paradox. It is a truism of politics. Two or three years ago a clerical member of the Prussian Herrenhaus attempted to overwhelm the German Chancellor by quoting at great length from a speech delivered by M. Bismarck some twenty years previously, in which he vehemently attacked the policy he had subsequently adopted as his own.

Nothing daunted by hearing the recent policy of his Government denounced so vehemently from the tribune in extracts selected from his former speech, Prince Bismarck listened attentively, and with a slight smile upon his strongly-marked features. When his assailant, with an air of triumph, had resumed his seat, Prince Bismarck said, "I have listened attentively to the speech which I delivered twenty years ago. I heard it with pleasure, and I am delighted to see that twenty years ago I understood the situation so well. At the present moment it would be all wrong, but then it was exactly what was needed. It is impossible now to secure the safety of the State except by departing from the tradition of that time."

Other statesmen have shown even less anxiety to justify the change of policy forced upon them by altered circumstances. The Duke of Wellington, when on one occasion he was challenged in the House of Lords with an apparent inconsistency, simply replied, with charming frankness, "I have changed my mind!"

The other day I saw at Mr. Theed's, the eminent sculptor, two splendid statues of the Right Hon. C. P. Villiers, M.P., which are to be erected at Manchester and Wolverhampton. Here was another instance of a change of policy, not by an individual, but by a whole nation. For thirteen years Mr. Villiers contended bravely in the House of Commons for the abolition of the Corn Laws He fought for the abandonment of the traditional policy of Great Britain in matters of trade, regarding with disdain the abusive attacks of a powerful majority. The nation was against him at first but the cause of right triumphed, the change was made, and, even in his lifetime, he is awarded the rare distinction of having statues erected in his honour by his grateful fellow-countrymen.

Every reform is more or less of a protest against the policy bequeathed to us by our ancestors—a revolt against the established traditions of the past. When the reform is accomplished men marvel at the opposition which it encountered. Of numberless instances take a case which was mentioned to me the other day, when we were talking of the universal satisfaction with which the abolition of the Concordat was regarded in Austro-Hungary. When the Council of the Vatican proclaimed the infallibility of the Holy Father the enunciation of that dogma effected a change in the relation between the Papacy and the Courts of Europe. Count Beust, at that time Chancellor of Austro-Hungary, recognised, with the keen perception of a statesman, that the time had come for breaking with the traditional policy of the past. Count Beust abolished the Concordat, and boldly initiated the new policy which the occasion required.

There is a significance about that last fact which should not be lost. The Sultan has not proclaimed in set terms the dogma of his infallibility, but he has done worse. At the Conference at Constantinople he asserted, for the first time for many years, his deliberate determination to defy the councils of all the Powers. Unanimously they urged him to accept the irreducible minima, and pertinaciously he refused. That refusal in itself

Some English Prejudices.

changed the whole situation. It was the Mussulman counterpart to the decree of the Vatican—an act of defiance to Europe and to civilisation. To some extent the English Government has recognised the impossibility of carrying out the old policy under such new conditions; but, unlike Count Beust, they have not boldly broken with the past, and annulled the unwritten Concordat which bound England to the Turk.

The reasons which led England to fight Russia in 1854 no longer exist. The whole situation is transformed. Is it not necessary to abandon the mistaken attempts to secure the peace of Europe by maintaining a government always and unavoidably at war with its own subjects? Peace, said Lord Derby, is the greatest of British interests. Why sacrifice it then by maintaining so obstinately a policy which has become an anachronism? Can you quick-moving Westerns, who invent the locomotive and talk by the telephone, be so absorbed in the trivial details of each day's business as to ignore two of the greatest facts of modern history? What are these facts? The first is the evident progress of Russia under our present Czar. The second is the establishment of the German Empire. By the first Russia gained new claims upon the sympathies of the civilised world. The second saved the Continent from the dread of the absolute predominance of Russia. The Turk is the only unprogressive Power left in Europe, and Turkish oppression is a worse menace to peace than "Russian aggression."

The Sick Man is sick unto death. England has tried to galvanise him into life; but the task exceeds even the resources of English wealth. And yet there are some who say, "Let him have one more chance!" But what is the meaning of this phrase? What can be the relations between the Turks and the Christians after the events of the last two years? But it is possible that the Turk may be spared. English diplomatic influence may succeed in maintaining the Turkish Empire against the determination of the whole of Russia. If so, while apparently adhering to the traditional policy of England, Lord Beaconsfield will have sacrificed the object for which that policy was invented, viz., the maintenance of a Power at Constantinople strong enough to keep peace in the East.

LETTER VIII.

RUSSIANS IN CENTRAL ASIA.

LETTER VIII.

RUSSIANS IN CENTRAL ASIA.

"THE Russians have as much right to conquer Central Asia as the English to seize India," observed a polite Englishman, the other day, evidently thinking that he had gone to the extreme of condescending kindness!

"May I be quite frank?" said I. "Well, it seems to me that we have a great deal better right in Central Asia than you have in India!" So startling a remark led to a long explanation. Perhaps Russian views on that point might be of some little interest in England. I scarcely hope to convince many of my readers, but I think it really is a duty to speak out one's mind sometimes, even when you feel yourself nothing but a poor exponent of the cause of truth. Consider me as a *pis-aller*. I don't mind. Personal considerations must be put aside under certain circumstances.

Letter VIII.

Well, now, as to the question of Central Asia. Turkestan is at our door. Neither precipitous mountain range nor stormy sea divided the Russian plain from the Tartar steppe. Our merchants have always traded with the Khanates; caravans have wended their way wearily over the monotonous expanse of the Central Asian desert for centuries. Every disturbance in Turkestan affected business in Russia. It became a necessity for the protection of the legitimate channels of commerce to establish some authority in these regions more respectable than the nomadic tribes who levied black mail with a threat of death. Step by step in the course of successive generations, the Russian civiliser encroached upon the Tartar savage. Evils tolerable at a distance are intolerable next door. Anarchy, objectionable anywhere, is unbearable when it infringes upon the frontiers of order. The extension of our sovereignty over the tribes of Tartary was the unavoidable consequence of our geographical position. Now: Was it so with you in India? You had to pass the Cape of Good Hope, and sail half round the world before you reached the land which you have subdued. The internal tranquillity of India had no bearing upon English interests. So you had at first no more right to conquer Hindostan than Russia has to annex Brazil.

Russia in Central Asia is without a rival as she is without an ally. If she did not establish order, toleration, and peace among those rude tribes on her frontiers the work would have remained undone to this day. In India, on the contrary, you have to justify your conquest not only against the reproaches of the conquered nations, but against the protests of the Dutch, the Portuguese, and the French, whom you ejected from the dominions which you had marked for your own. Russia in Central Asia does the police work of an enormous expanse of thinly-populated, poverty-stricken land. She taxes the peasants of Saratoff and Kieff to maintain order in Khokand and Tashkent. The Administration spends two roubles in collecting one. The English people, I think, pay nothing for the government of India. The Hindoos had to pay the expense of their conquest, and they defray at this moment the whole charges of the foreign administration which is maintained in India by English bayonets.

India is rich. Central Asia is poor. The whole of the revenue raised in Turkestan is not half a million in the year. In India you raise more than fifty millions.

There was little to plunder in Tashkent—much less than the English nabobs found in one of the great cities of Northern India.

There was more need for Russians in Central Asia than there was for Englishmen in Bengal. The Tartar of the steppe needs a policeman much more than the timid Bengaleee. India had a civilization of her own, the splendour of which is attested to this day by those architectural remains to which Mr. Fergusson has devoted such patient genius and so many years of unremitting toil. The Khanates were hotbeds of savagery and fanaticism. The condition of these Tartar States was unspeakably bad. Arminius Vambery is one of the greatest Russian-haters in the world, but he admits that our soldiers have made it possible for Europeans to live in Bokhara. Formerly, Vambery himself could only visit the city disguised as a Mohammedan. Mr. Schuyler says :—" The rule of Russia is on the whole beneficial to the natives, and it would be manifestly unjust to them to withdraw her protection and leave them to anarchy and to the unbridled rule of fanatical despots."

We do not grudge England her Indian Empire, but when we are reproached with territorial greed for having annexed some deserts close to our frontiers we have a right to ask England to look to herself. India is yours, and improved by your rule. May it remain yours for ever! But the happy possessors of that magnificent Empire should not reproach us for our poor Tartar steppes. To understand the difficulties of our position in Central Asia, look not to India, but to your West African Settlements. You hold territories there which do not pay their expenses; they involve occasional wars which you wisely undertake without humbly asking the benediction of Russia or any other Power. Nevertheless you do not give them up; you even extend them from time to time without asking for our leave. Your keeping these provinces is perhaps more generous than giving them up, but there are Russians cruel enough to read with a little smile of your troubles with the King of Ashantee when they remember with what admirable fortitude you bore our difficulties with the Khan of Khiva.

In Central Asia Russians suppress the slave-trade as you do on the African coast, although at the first your views upon the subject were less philanthropic—if I remember well. Wherever the Russian flag flies freedom to the slave is guaranteed. If England had but joined us in our crusade against the Turk, the last stronghold of the slave-trade in Europe would have already ceased to exist. English people have no right to ignore this phase of the question when they can refer to such an unimpeachable "Statement of Facts on Turkey and the Slave Trade" as that written by Mr. F. W. Chesson, whose name is familiar to everyone as the energetic and fearless defender of the oppressed. One of the numerous complaints against us Russians is that we do not open the markets of Central Asia to the manufactures of all the world. Were you free-traders when you first conquered India? The East India Company, I believe, held as strict a monopoly as ever existed in the world.

About the wretched Khivan business, on which everybody, especially the most ignorant, feels himself competent to speak with authority, permit me to state categorically a few facts. We promised (I really do not know why) not to annex that questionable paradise, and we have not broken our pledge. The Khan reigns in all his glory in Khiva at this hour. But promises of that kind, as English experience goes, cannot always be kept as faithfully as we have kept ours. The illustrious Burke, in the House of Commons in 1783, said that "from Mount Imaus to Cape Comorin there is not a single prince or State with which the English Government had come into contact which they had not sold. There was not a single treaty which they ever made with a native State or prince which they had not broken." But we admit, in spite of Burke's severe blame, that, though probably only yielding to the necessity of her position, England, at all events, has given to India the blessings of a civilised and stable Government. Is Russia not entitled to the same amount of credit?

Even Lord Beaconsfield views with no mistrust the advance of Russia in Asia—that is, if you can believe what he said not so very long ago from his place in Parliament—where, I suppose, he speaks with more precision than after dinner at the Guildhall.* The Premier used the following words—which I quote the more gladly because it is so seldom that I can appeal to his testimony:— "I think that Asia is large enough for the destinies of Russia and England. Far from looking forward with alarm to the development of Russia in Central Asia, I see no reason why they should not conquer Tartary any more than why England should not have conquered India."

Why should English Turkophiles out-Herod Herod?

* I have read somewhere that in an ecclesiastical trial before the Privy Council, an advocate, wishing to fix a particular meaning upon an incriminated passage, said: "Either that is the meaning of the passage, my lords, or it has no meaning at all." "I am no theologian," replied the Lord Justice, "but is it not possible that the passage may have no meaning at all?" So I would say to those who try to find out the meaning of Lord Beaconsfield's speeches; but I come to that conclusion only because of my frequent visits to England. Foreigners are not always able to understand the difference between the real and the apparent value of the speeches of English statesmen.

LETTER IX.

MR. FORBES' ARTICLE.

LETTER IX.

MR. FORBES' ARTICLE.

[*The article contributed by Mr. Forbes to the "Nineteenth Century," on "Russians, Turks, and Bulgarians, at the Seat of War," occasioned so much controversy, that a Russian view of the question may, perhaps, not be considered as out of place.*]

"LIGHT, more light!" murmured Goethe on his deathbed. We Russians are in more urgent need of light in order to live. M. Aksakoff last month said, "Light! light! as much light as possible—that is what Russia now requires. In light are health, force, power, and the possibility of recovery." That light, he said, comes to us chiefly from abroad, and we owe most of it to two English correspondents—Mr. M'Gahan and Mr. Forbes. In the name of the whole Russian people, which even in its remotest villages has read and re-read their letters, M. Aksakoff thanked these Englishmen, not only for their sympathy, but still more for "the calm, bitter truths" which they had spoken.

Since M. Aksakoff spoke Mr. Forbes has published an article in the *Nineteenth Century*. He praises my countrymen, and I thank him for doing them justice. He criticises their administration, and I thank him still more for his candour in assisting us to remedy our short-comings. He severely condemns some of our military commanders, and, if true, these things cannot be too plainly exposed. We are not infallible, we Russians, as is the Holy Father, whose infallibility, however, has not prevented him from sympathizing with the infidels against whom his no less infallible predecessors preached crusades. Like other nations, we make mistakes, and no one can do us better service than by pointing them out. Mr. Forbes might have spared us a few sneers; but these we can overlook. As a Russian I do not complain.

But as a Slav I protest against the way in

which he abuses the Bulgarians. I am indignant at these virulent attacks upon the feeble and those who have no helper. Better—far better—that he should denounce us and spare them. We, at least, are strong, but they, the weak, the wretched, the oppressed—is it manly to heap insults upon such as these? They cannot reply. They cannot resent his abuse, no matter how undeserved. And it is undeserved! Mr. Forbes has never been for a single day in Bulgaria under Turkish rule. He has only seen Bulgarians after the Pasha, the Zaptieh, the Tcherkess, and the Bashi-Bazouk had fled "bag and baggage" before our liberating army. How is he to know what they suffered? Mr. M'Gahan, who visited Bulgaria when the Turk was in possession, gives a very different account of the happiness of the Bulgarian. Mr. Forbes has never been across the Balkans. He has never been near the scene of the atrocities. But he admits that the Turks are "persistent, indomitable barbarians." He says they "wield the axe and the chopper of ruthless savages," that they mutilate the dead and torture the wounded. The Bulgarians are at the mercy of these men. Unless they become renegades, their complaints and testimonies are not accepted by the Turkish tribunals. Power which elsewhere is believed to be too vast to be entrusted to the most civilised of men, in Bulgaria is exercised by the Ottoman barbarians, and from their will there is no appeal.

In Russia we sometimes indignantly say that the heart of England is eaten up with love of gold. Surely that cannot be true. Still, what is Mr. Forbes' argument, so eagerly repeated by Turkophiles? Is it not based upon a belief that money is everything? The Bulgarian, unlike "Devonshire Giles," has more than nine shillings a week. Therefore he needs no liberation! His wives and daughters are at the mercy of the Zaptieh. But is woman's honour really nothing compared with solid gold?

Russians are pretty good judges of courage. Well, there is not one Russian, who fought side by side with the Bulgarians, who does not praise their courage and their simple, determined way of meeting death. Mr. Forbes himself, in his description of the Shipka battles, showed that he shared

Russian views upon this matter. A certain way of sacrificing life is a very charming argument in favour of the moral character of the nation.

The result of Turkish oppression on the character of the Bulgarians is not favourable. But even that, in Mr. Forbes' eyes, tells in favour of the Turks, as the Bulgarians are so degraded they are not worth saving. What, then, are we to say of Him who came to seek and to save that which was lost? If four centuries of Turkish misrule have brutalised these poor Bulgarians, is it not time that it ceased? Permit me to extract some words of Earl Russell's I find in a pamphlet, given to me by Messrs. Zancoff and Balabanoff, the Bulgarian delegates. He wrote: "It would indeed be a hopeless case for mankind if despotism were thus allowed to take advantage of its own wrong, and to bring the credence of its own crimes as the title-deeds of its right. It would be, indeed, a strange perversion of justice if absolute Governments might say, 'Look how ignorant, base, false, and cruel our people have become under our sway; therefore we have a right to retain them in eternal subjection, in everlasting slavery.'" Yet this "strange perversion of justice" is employed in order to damage the cause of the Southern Slavs.

The Russian administration, according to Mr. Forbes, is so very corrupt that a French correspondent has employed himself in collecting and authenticating cases of peculation with a view to its future publication. If that French correspondent does his work thoroughly he will be entitled to the gratitude of the Russian people. There are corrupt contractors I suppose in Roumania, as there have always been in all wars, and perhaps always will be, and we are more interested in their detection and punishment even than Mr. Forbes. But it is a mistake to attach so exaggerated importance to such stories. Gambetta's contractors sold the new levies paper-soled boots. Great fortunes were made by dishonest purveyors to the army of the Potomac, and the English army in the Crimea was not too well served at the commencement of the war. Is there no bribing in England—not even among the detective police? Are "tips" and "commissions" known only in Russia? But this is beside the question. If Mr. Forbes will substantiate his accusations we will thank him for revealing the weak places in our armour. The charge that Russian officers are willing to betray their country for a bribe is too serious to be made in such vague terms. It ought either to be supported with details, dates, and names, or it ought not to be made at all. Vagueness in a case like this is simply cruel to the whole Russian army. At present it cannot be investigated; but, as an act of simple justice, Mr. Forbes should so far overcome his "melancholy" as to enable the Russian nation to punish these traitors.

One word more about our officers. I am not a military authority, and do not meddle with these things. Englishmen, of course, who never have any little difficulties between the Horse Guards and the War Office, and who select their Commander-in-Chief not because he is a Royal Highness but solely because he is the greatest military genius in the land, cannot understand the existence of such a thing as favouritism in the army. But it is not necessary to resort to such an argument to explain the absence of those Generals named by Mr. Forbes from the seat or war. Todleben, for instance, who, according to Mr. Forbes, was only sent for as a last resource, was engaged at the beginning of the campaign in putting the Baltic ports in a position to resist the anticipated attack of the English fleet. Kaufmann remained in Turkestan because he of all men was best fitted for the arduous and responsible work of governing Central Asia. Only foreigners consider Turkestan a sinecure or a Paradise. As for the "neglected retirement" of Bariatinsky, it is the usual accusation that the Bariatinskys are in too great favour at Court. Both charges cannot be true, and one may be left to answer the other. Kotzebue is in command at Warsaw, nor is the position one to be despised. As for the lion-hearted Tchernayeff, to whom I am heartily glad to see Mr. Forbes pays a well-merited word of praise, I regret as much as any one that he was not permitted to take a prominent part in the campaign. But can Englishmen not suspect the reason why the General who fought against Turkey when Russia was at peace, is not appointed at once to high command now that Russia is at war? No one fought in Servia without first resigning his commission in the Russian army, and diplomatic susceptibilities might be offended if the Russian Government were so completely to condone the part played by Tchernayeff in the Servian War.

In conclusion, let me say that Mr. Forbes, as unfortunately so many of our crities, generalises too hastily from imperfect *data*. He jumps to erroneous conclusions, and prefers his own theories to the well-attested evidence of trustworthy eye-witnesses. M. Aksakoff thanked him for stating "calm and bitter truths." The statements in his last article may be "bitter," but they certainly are not "calm," and many of them as little deserve the name of "truths."

LETTER X.

M. KATKOFF AND THE "MOSCOW GAZETTE.

LETTER X.

M. KATKOFF AND THE "MOSCOW GAZETTE."

[*Foreign newspapers frequently quote as representatives of Russian opinion such journals as the "Golos," the "St. Petersburg Exchange Gazette," and others, which are by no means faithful exponents of the national sentiment. It is to the "Moscow Gazette" that undoubtedly belongs the honour of being the most representative Russian newspaper, a fact which should not be lost sight of when references are made to the Russian Press.*]

THE *Moscow Gazette* is the *Times* of Russia. In one sense, but not in another. It is the first paper in the Empire, but it leads rather than follows public opinion. The *Times* veers with the times. The *Moscow Gazette* adheres to its own views. The *Times* is impersonal, anonymous.

The *Moscow Gazette* is M. Katkoff, and M. Katkoff is the *Moscow Gazette*. He has his colleagues, but his individuality permeates the paper.

The *Moscow Gazette* belongs to the University of Moscow, but M. Katkoff has leased it for twelve years for a sum of more than £120,000, payable in twelve annual instalments. It enjoys a monopoly of the Government advertisements. Its circulation and influence, always great, have received a remarkable increase through the national movement which resulted in the war.

Few men have influenced more deeply the course of events in Russia since the Emancipation than the quondam Professor of Philology in the University of Moscow. A Russian of the Russians, married to Princess Shalikoff, daughter of a Russian poet, he was at one time so ardent an admirer of England and the English that his friends reproached him for his Anglo-mania, and even now it is his journal which does most justice to the English nation in relation to the war in the East. A brilliant author, a learned professor, a fearless journalist, M. Katkoff's chief distinction is due to the fact that he more than any man incarnated the national inspirations at three crises in Russian history.

It was in 1863 that he first attracted the attention of Russia. In that year the determination of the Poles that half of Russia should be included in the limits of the Poland to which a Constitution was about to be granted brought them into violent collision with the Russian Government. All the Powers of Europe began to intermeddle in the matter. "You must do this; you must not do that," and so on. The despatches came pouring in from this Court and from that, until even little Portugal and barbarous Turkey ventured to send us their prescriptions for pacifying Poland! Russians felt profoundly humiliated, and not a little indignant. "Were we not to be masters in our own house? Were we to be treated as if we were the vassals of the West?" These angry questionings filled every breast; and, amid the irritation occasioned by the intermeddling of the Foreign Courts, everything was forgotten but a stern resolve to vindicate the national independence. At that crisis in our history M. Katkoff came boldly to the front, embodied the thoughts of millions in his fiery articles, and gave voice and utterance to the patriotic enthusiasm of every Russian. When the storm had passed, and all danger of war was averted by the adoption of the independent policy which he had so vigorously advocated, the intrepid spokesman of the national sentiment occupied the highest place in the esteem of his countrymen ever attained by any journalist in Russia before or since. A public subscription was raised, and M. Katkoff was presented, in the name of thousands of sympathisers throughout the Empire, with a massive silver figure of a soldier in the old Russian uniform, holding proudly aloft a standard, bearing " Honour of Russia " as its inscription.

Some years later M. Katkoff came once more to the front. The question of classical education then excited intense interest throughout Russia, and the *Moscow Gazette* led the van of the fight, which resulted in the complete victory of the classical party. As one result of this success "The Lyceum of the Grand Duke Nicholas" was founded at Moscow, in honour of the late Czarewitch. M. Katkoff and M. Leontieff, his *alter ego* —and a very distinguished scholar—were associated at first in the superintendence of the new institution. Since the death of the latter—which was lamented throughout Russia as a national loss—M. Katkoff has discharged alone the duties of president.

The third great crisis in which M. Katkoff and the *Moscow Gazette* did good service to the Russian cause was in the Slavonic movement of last year. M. Katkoff has never been identified with the Slavophile party. But when the Servian war awakened the national enthusiasm M. Katkoff threw himself heart and soul into the Slavonic cause. He guided, directed, and sustained more than any single man the tumultuous current of Russian opinion. The *Moscow Gazette* became once more the exponent of the national conviction, and to this hour it maintains the honourable position of the leading journal of Russia.

M. Katkoff publishes not only the *Moscow Gazette* but also a monthly literary organ—the Russian *Messenger*. He is famous throughout Europe for his incisive style and his vigorous hard-hitting. The courage with which he has assailed abuses has not prevented the appointment of his daughter, Miss Barbe Katkoff, as demoiselle d' Honneur to her Majesty the Empress.

It is impossible to do an author justice in a translation, but some idea of M. Katkoff's method of handling a subject may be formed from the following rough condensation of the leading article in the *Moscow Gazette* on Mr. Forbes' contribution to the *Nineteenth Century* on "Russians, Turks, and Bulgarians":—

After mentioning the fact that Mr. Forbes has contributed an article to the *Nineteenth Century*, the *Moscow Gazette* takes notice of his remarks on the valour of the Russian soldiers, and the faults of the Russian administration, observing that we ourselves know our shortcomings, and fortunately our mistakes are capable of an easy remedy. His praises of the Russian soldier are especially grateful, because the qualities which he eulogises are not the product of a few months or years of drill, but they are characteristic of the very nature of the Russian nation. When Mr. Forbes speaks of the Russians we accept his testimony as that of an honest military man; but when he proceeds to speak of the Turks and the Bulgarians he loses completely both his self-control and his conscience. After referring to Mr. Forbes' testimony about the Bulgarians, the article points out that, according to the universal concurrent testimony of all English travellers and officials, the Bulgarian, of all the inhabitants of Europe, was the most patient and industrious. As the soil of Bulgaria is naturally very fertile, the application of the industry of the Bulgarian naturally brings wealth. But, because this patient worker begins to show signs of improvement, because after paying his heavy taxes he finds some money left to build schools for the education of his children, Mr. Forbes curses him! "Behold what they have got!" he cries. "How can we speak of their oppression? Is it not evident that life under the Turkish yoke cannot be very unpleasant? Even although the prosperous Bulgarian who has roses in his garden and grapes over his door is ruined now and then by the Zaptieh and the Tcherkess, what does it signify? Devonshire Giles would be glad to exchange places with the victim of Turkish oppression!" So says Mr. Forbes, and the phrase undoubtedly looks very nice in print; but if it were possible to make such an experiment it would be necessary to state to Devonshire Giles a few facts which perhaps might make him less desirous to enjoy the roses and the grapes of Bulgaria. For instance, if he were told that he would have to be not only the slave of every Turkish official, but that every Turk could violate the honour of his wife and daughters, and that he himself would be liable to be treated like a dog and hanged without redress, does Mr. Forbes think that Devonshire Giles would be so eager to exchange his lot with that of the Bulgarian and take his chance of the atrocities which Mr. Forbes seems to have forgotten, but which Mr. Baring and Mr. Schuyler described only last year?

"Is it possible to make Mr. Forbes understand that it is not the climate, nor the soil, nor the industry of the Bulgarians, with its resultant roses and grapes, that Russia wishes to change, but the treatment to which the inhabitants are subjected, which, under the Turk, is no better than that of giaours and dogs?

"The Turks have only done one act for which they can be accused of humanity, and for that solitary exception to their usual savage brutality they are blamed by Mr. Forbes! They ought, according to this Englishman, to have devastated Bulgaria before the Russian advance. Philanthropists might scream, but wise men would have approved of their action in laying a whole province in ashes and driving the inhabitants into exile! And because they did not perpetrate that crowning atrocity Mr. Forbes upbraids the Bulgarians for their ingratitude for the 'generosity' of the Turks!

"What can be the reason for Mr. Forbes' hatred of this whole race of wretched, despised, poor, Christian people? The reason is not far to seek. It was these Bulgarians whose sufferings occasioned the war. That war can only be terminated by their securing complete independence from the claws of the barbarian. An independent Bulgaria means a weakened Turkey—a prospect which is distasteful to Englishmen. Hence this article, which has been received as a Godsend by the *Cologne Gazettes* and the *Pall Mall Gazettes* of the Continent, who even accept his praises of the Russians as a proof of his impartiality when he abuses the Bulgarians and eulogises the Turks."

So far the *Moscow Gazette*. M. Katkoff shares the mistake of many of my countrymen that an Englishman is so naturally biassed in favour of the Turks that he resorts to this bias as the easiest explanation of Mr. Forbes' animus against the Bulgarians. Had M. Katkoff been in England lately he would have known that a great number of the very best Englishmen are longing as earnestly as himself for the final extinction of the Ottoman Empire.

O. K.

www.ingramcontent.com/pod-product-compliance
Lightning Source LLC
Chambersburg PA
CBHW020100170426
43199CB00009B/355